Blue Bus to Sere

A MEMOIR

by Judith Zottoli

ISBN-13: 978-1479351169
ISBN-10: 1479351164

Designed by Jon Case
Published by Judith Zottoli through CreateSpace.com
Published in the United States of America

Judith Zottoli, 2010

Introduction

Because the Italian side of my family did not accept me, I always felt a part of me was missing. My heart, my soul and my spirit told me there was something yet to find. I wanted to know who they were, how they thought and where I fit into their world.

So, my journey, which ends on a blue bus to Serre, Italy, where my grandfather Zottoli was born, led me to discover that my Italian-self had been there all along, that I belonged there. When I arrived, I told anyone who would listen that my name is Zottoli, that my *nonno*, grandfather, came from Serre. I was also inspired to express my feelings in poetry, which I have included throughout the story.

My memories and those passed down to me by family members are presented here in hopes they capture something for future generations of our family.

Acknowledgements

I want to thank my family members who contributed their memories and photos.

Also, my thanks to the B&N Writing Group in Asheville, NC for their critical suggestions and support.

Thanks to Jon Case for his help in publishing this memoir.

The Courting

Sparks must have flown the first time Jeanne Macomber, a fair English maiden, and Robert Angelo Zottoli, Bob, a hot, handsome Italian, met. I would love to have known them during that time. Mom, a student at Byrn Mawr, the same college her stepmother and sister had attended, returned home for the summer in Squantum, Massachusetts. Dad was studying law at Boston University Law School and worked part-time for his father as a stone-mason.

They belonged to two different worlds, two different backgrounds. In the 1930s, discrimination against Italians was widespread in our area of the country. In the seventeenth century immigrants from Italy had been respected. They were generally musicians, educators and artists. In the nineteenth century, Italian Catholic immigrants were restricted to lower class, blue-collar jobs for the most part. Formal education was unusual. Because my grandmother and grandfather Zottoli were not formally educated, they set very high standards for their four children. Three of them graduated from college. Sadly, my father, trying to distance himself from his heritage, did not learn to speak Italian, and thus was not able to pass it down to me and my siblings.

The two separate worlds that my folks came from collided. Both sets of parents objected to their relationship, but the young couple persisted, and the stark difference in family cultures caused a monumental clash.

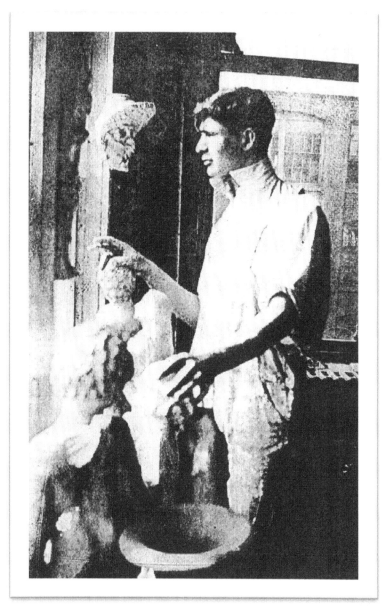

Robert Angelo Zottoli in his father's studio. 1930

Grandfather Macomber, my mother's father, was a gynecologist who treated infertility in the 1930s and 1940s. He was a WASP, every inch a white, Anglo-Saxon, Protestant. He and my grandmother lived in an English Tudor, waterfront home in a very nice section of Squantum, Massachusetts, an island-like peninsula jutting into Quincy Bay. Mom was living with them that summer, taking her German exams at Harvard Summer School. Judge and Mrs. Zottoli lived next door in their fancy summer home. Judge Zottoli, Uncle Joe, had the proper connections to rise above the fray and become a judge. Both imposing homes sat close to each other on unlikely small lots. My father's sister, Clara, and her husband Fred were "vacationing" in the Judge's home. My Father, Bob, was visiting them. Boating and swimming were literally in the back yard.

My blond, blue-eyed Mom was quiet and slender. On the summer evening that the sparks flew, she had come home from school, but could not get her key to turn in the lock. Frustrated, she went next door to Judge Zottoli's house and knocked. The Judge's niece answered the door. "Let me get my brother Bob," she said. The judge and his wife were away on a vacation cruise, so their niece, her husband and nephew were house-sitting. A tall, dark, handsome young man, a struggling lawyer, came to the door. Mom and Dad were immediately attracted to each other.

After trying and failing to get in through various windows and doors, he tried the key in the front door lock. It worked like a charm. The next night, she couldn't get the key to turn. Again she asked him for help, and according to my father, the door flew open. She felt foolish to ask for help again, but the desire to see him overpowered her embarrassment. The following night they went on their first date. Honeysuckle and Chanel No. 5 wafted with moonbeams as my mother rowed my father in the moonlight over Quincy Bay.

At the end of the summer, Mom went back to Byrn Mawr College to finish her senior year. She said that she found the intellectual snobs on campus much more intimidating than her studies. She told me and my siblings many years later that sometime during that year, she and my father secretly married. They honeymooned in a bedbug infested hotel in New York's Greenwich Village. Before she returned to college, her parents warned her that they did not like her dating an Italian Catholic. Her father explained to her that it was not Bob, personally, to whom he objected, but he thought the cultures were too different, that she would regret the marriage later

Mom's continual grumpiness and foul moods wore Grampa down, and he finally agreed to allow a wedding. Little did he know they were already married. There was one condition: that he examine Bob for infertility. Dr. Macomber connected Italians with disease. My Dad's response was simple: "I'll agree to an examination by your father, but I'll examine him first."

The engagement was announced March 2, 1938, at a tea at the home of Dr. and Mrs. Donald Macomber. The house was decorated with daffodils, tulips and lilacs. The passion and color complemented the tea pourers, members from both families. An early summer wedding was announced.

Mom and Dad were married in Grammy's garden by a Protestant minister. This upset Dad's parents, but they did come. Mother was neither Italian nor Catholic. My parents' marriage was not recognized by the Catholic Church, because they would not agree to bring their children up as Catholics. This incident was never discussed openly in my family. In spite of the tensions, the wedding took place in early June. Grammy Macomber worked her magic in her gardens. Pink peonies mixed with wide-brimmed pastel hats, long summer dresses and white gloves hid any strain between families. Live violin music drifted over the garden and into the sparkling ocean beyond.

In the early years of their marriage, Mom and Dad lived in the basement apartment of her parents' house. Dad struggled to establish a law practice in the Quincy area and was seldom at home. Mom took care of my older brother Tony and shortly thereafter, me. Grammy Macomber adhered to the popular child rearing philosophies of that time. She advised my mother not to shower us with love, to withhold affection. My sweet Mom did not listen. She would escape Grammy's eyes to the basement apartment below and cover us with kisses and hugs.

Mom did not want to raise her children as she had been. Her father was a strict disciplinarian to Mom and her five brothers and sisters, each two years apart in age. When Mom turned 13, Grampa decided his children should have lockers and inspection every day at five o'clock. He went from locker to locker checking for neatness, and then moved on to inspect each child's bed. Demerits meant a decrease in allowance.

This sternness came, in part, from his service in World War I. As an added incentive for his children to comply with his rules, Grampa Macomber often drove the family in his Model T, "Tin Lizzie," through the poor sections of Boston. He said to the children, "Just know that you could be living in the poor house at any time."

Mom loved taking care of her children, which helped pass the lonely days in an apartment void of sunshine. Small basement windows below and parents, who watched over her a little too closely from above, could be trying. Sunday became a day of worship at home for our family. My Father, whom we called Papa, was always at home on Sundays. We had dinner together, a roast and all the fixings. Papa always carved the roast. Good food, funny papers and laughter. We lived there for two and a half years.

Judith and Tony Zottoli, 1944

Ma Mere

Sweet Ma Mere,
Eyes blue as the sea,
Hair white as the snow,
Meets all with such glee.

Non-judgmental,
So full of life,
Eager to know you,
A dedicated wife.

Sweet Ma Mere,
How you soothe my soul,
Tell me more stories,
From years ago.

Discuss Henry James,
Watch Soap of the day,
Show me your paintings,
Make life O.K.

Sweet Ma Mere,
I love and adore,
Meet me always,
I implore.

Jeanne Macomber Zottoli, 1938

Nana and Grampa Zottoli

Mom and Dad moved twenty-five times between 1938 and Mom's death in 2011. We always thought it was Dad who initiated the moves, but my mother admitted to me in later years, that she was the one. I caught her bug and have made eleven moves. Pa would say, "Call Henry Underhill." Henry owned a moving company and moved us each time; furniture hanging out the back of an old blue truck transported us from one location to another.

In 1946, when I was five years old, we moved to Quincy to live with my father's parents, Nana and Grampa Zottoli, because my father found it too difficult to practice law in Quincy while living in Scituate. There were five of us, my mother and father, my brother Tony, seven years old, my sister Joan, three years old, and me. My mother was pregnant with Steven.

This was the house my father grew up in with two sisters and one brother, who died of tuberculosis at the age of forty. When they first moved into the neighborhood in the 1920's, they were the only Italian family. At first, they were discriminated against, but over the years, as people got to know the Zottolis, they were loved and accepted. When we moved into the home in the 1940's we felt no discrimination.

Nana, a large-bosomed woman, was about twenty years younger than Grampa. Her parents had emigrated from Italy. She always wore a nylon dress with a busy print, a full-size apron, and black shoes

Robert Angelo, Clara, and Arthur.
Anthony and Josephine Zottoli's children, 1915

with ties and fat heels. Her hair was pulled severely
back in a tight bun. The smells emanating from her
kitchen were wonderful. There is a dent in the wall of

that old house where my father was back-handed for saying, "This is the best meal I have ever had," in front of company. But Nana had a good sense of humor, and shook all over when she laughed.

Easter at Nana and Grampa Zottoli's house, 1946
Back row, Jeanne Zottoli, Nana Zottoli, Anthony M. Zottoli
Front row, Cousin Frank, Judith, Joan, Tony, Unknown woman.

Grampa was short in stature, balding and had a mustache. He was a stone mason and sculptor. He and his brothers formed a company in Boston, where they made cement statues of the Virgin Mary, rabbits, lions and columns, to name a few. His work kept him very busy, so we saw little of him at home. He enjoyed painting oil pictures of flowers and ships at sea. He emigrated from Italy with some of his family when he was thirteen to join his father.

My brother, Tony, and I spent most of our time outdoors, me tagging along after him. Once, we walked on ice cakes in the bay. We also went on treks to Moon Island which was connected to the mainland by a causeway. There was a sewage processing plant there with large indoor and outdoor storage vats. I can plainly remember standing on the edge and peering down into the large vats outside. The island was a considerable distance from our home. I'm sure with all the confusion in the house, Mom didn't know of our forays.

I have few memories of that time in my grandparents' home as I was only five, but some remain beautiful and others distant, dark and mysterious. I remember Grampa singing in the garden early in the morning, before the dew was off the grass, as he worked the soil with his bare hands and feet. We were not allowed in the garage full of statues of lions, columns, rabbits and other mysterious forms. I also remember the beautiful flowers Grampa painted on oyster shells to be used for ashtrays and sold on Cape Cod. His oil paintings adorned the walls in most rooms of the house. I remember starting to go down into the dark cellar once, but stopped. Tony told me there was a cement vat where Grampa made wine, which was put into wooden barrels. I have a vivid memory of him shaving with a straight razor in the kitchen after sharpening it on a leather strap.

The entire year we lived with Nana and Grampa was difficult for Mom. She was submerged in the culture of another family who initially resented that she was neither Catholic nor Italian. The chaos created by having five more people, three of them small children, got to be too much for Nana, so she would often leave to visit her sister. Mom was lonely and didn't feel accepted. My dad was busy with his law practice. I felt the same coldness from my grandmother as did Mom. I have no memory of being hugged by either grandparent.

Tony, Joan, Steve, and Judith Zottoli, 1947

The summer of that year, we went to live in one of Mom's parents' cottages in Maine. At that time my brother Steven was born and Mom refused to go back to live at Nana and Grampa's when my father proposed the idea. Instead, my parents returned and rented a house in Squantum, Massachusetts, a part of Quincy. My grandfather Zottoli, who was in his early seventies, passed away at this time. Our Nana went to live with her daughter, Clara, and her husband Fred. She was in her early fifties and lived in Clara's house until she died at ninety-five.

Visiting Auntie Clara

When I was eight or nine years old, I remember going to visit my father's sister, Auntie Clara. As we drove the five or six miles from our rented house in Squantum to Greenleaf Street in Quincy, my face was pressed to the car window. I saw the houses get larger and fancier.

Aunt Clara and Uncle Fred Costanza
At their cottage in maine, 1990s

I was nervous as we neared their large, cold house. This is where Nana had moved to live with her daughter Clara, her husband, and their two children, Mary Elaine and Freddie. We entered the house through what had been the servant's kitchen on the first floor. It had become Nana's domain; she did all the cooking there. She was usually cooking some Italian delight with peppers, onions, zucchini, summer squash, spaghetti, liver or chicken, or some combination of them. I remember the taste of what we called *sufreta*, liver, onions, squash and tomato sauce. I loved *frishedella*, scrambled eggs and tomato sauce. My father had the secret to Nana's spaghetti sauce and passed it on to me.

On occasion we had lunch at the kitchen table, but were told to be quiet as Uncle Fred, a family physician, was seeing patients on the other side of the door. Sometimes he would join us for lunch. He was rotund with a big nose and penetrating brown eyes. He tended to be brusque and all business. The rest of the first floor held his office, the waiting room, and an elegant formal dining room in which I have no memory of having had a meal. The Thanksgivings that we attended were at the home of my father's youngest sister, Kay.

Auntie Clara was attractive, slim, wore her hair pulled back in a chignon and wore chic clothes. I never saw her wear slacks. She did a lot of charity and society work. She had a good heart and sense of humor, but I felt a coldness from her too. I did not see my cousins Mary Elaine and Freddie very much until a later age, because they attended private schools. I remember one occasion when Auntie Clara took me and cousin Freddie on an outing to Cape Cod. Freddie was hilarious and we laughed and laughed. I have always felt close to him. I didn't know Mary Elaine until later, when we moved to Maine.

There were two staircases in Auntie's house. The back one was very steep and narrow and led to Nana's apartment on the third floor. She went up and down these stairs twice a day until well into her nineties. The grand staircase went from the waiting room to the second floor and was covered with oriental rugs. At the landing, half way up, were beautiful geraniums tended by Nana. The bedrooms and living room were on the second floor and plush carpet made me feel I was walking on air. A collection of Hummel figurines fascinated me. On occasion I sat on a leather couch, which crinkled under me. Uncle Fred sat in a leather chair and filled the room with cigar smoke. Two dachshunds ran in and out. Three of the bedrooms looked unlived in.

Nana lived on the third floor. I loved to be up there, but was only invited twice that I remember. The walls were covered with Grampa Zottoli's art work, oil paintings of ships, seas, flowers and faraway places. Books were held with hand-carved bookends. How I wanted a piece of that family heritage, but I would not ask. That was not done. Nana never offered me one, even in later years. I have a panel of oil paintings now that my mother gave me. There were four panels that my grandfather made for my mother, but never finished.

The Geranium

In Summer
Pink, red, rose
Geraniums
Adorn my deck,
And those balconies
Of my ancestors.

In Winter,
A delicate, pink
Geranium
Lifts my spirits,
Meditates my soul,
Transforming me
In time and place.

Visiting Auntie Kay

Kay Hansen, my father's youngest sister, is still alive. She's in her nineties and still beautiful, inside and out. She is down to earth, talented and one of the few Zottolis who has treated me and my immediate family with genuine love and affection. Perhaps because she married a non-Catholic, non-Italian Danish man, she understood how we felt.

Kay worked as a school librarian for many years. In her younger years she had long, wavy chestnut hair, large brown eyes and was tall. Her husband, Uncle Eddie, was a World War II veteran. On his return from the Pacific, he suffered mental and physical ailments from active duty. He was an alcoholic and, ironically, a beer salesman. Uncle Eddie was the sweetest man. He had a gentle, loving way and everyone was fond of him.

Their first child, Petey, was born severely retarded. As he got older, he had to be secured to a chair, because he kicked with great strength at anyone who came near him. Auntie Kay had bruises all over her body. He could not walk or talk, but could only grunt and scream for food. She was told she should institutionalize him, but could or would not. He died from a weak heart at the age of eight. Their second son, Donnie, was not afflicted. Nana often visited on overnight stays to help with Petey.

Our family spent Thanksgivings at Auntie Kay's along with Nana and Grampa Zottoli. Aunt Clara and her family went to her husband Fred's family on Thanksgiving. The food preparation went on for a week and produced a sumptuous feast. Along with the usual turkey and all the trimmings, we had lasagna, *melanzana,* eggplant casserole; *zucca,* butternut squash; and *pepona,* sausage stuffing. After dinner, the women gathered in the kitchen to wash dishes and the men took naps.

Thanksgiving at Auntie Kay Hansen's, 1947
Left to right, Tony Zottoli, Gaga (Grampa) Hansen, Uncle Edward Hansen,
Unknown, Joan Zottoli, Auntie Kay Hansen, Petey Hansen, Grampa Zottoli,
Nana Zottoli, Jeanne Zottoli, Judith Zottoli, Steven Zottoli

When I was eleven, Auntie Kay invited me to spend a week with her and her family. My visit was loving. She found another girl my age in the neighborhood and we walked and talked together. The neighborhood was Adams Shore, part of Quincy. Many years later, I became the Branch Librarian at Adams Shore Library. It was a middle-to-lower-class neighborhood. Kay and Eddie were given their home by his father who then lived in the apartment upstairs.

During that visit, I ate baloney, mayo and pickles for lunch every day. I remember telling my aunt there was a man and woman screaming at each other next door. She assured me it was all right, that he drank too much and that they often argued. Uncle Eddie would be gone all day, mostly to bars, but was home at night sleeping in his chair. I food-shopped and did errands with Auntie. It was a special visit with her. For the first time, I felt accepted by someone in our family.

With the exception of my closeness to Auntie Kay and my cousins, Mary Elaine and Freddie Costanza, I did not feel accepted by the other Zottolis. I didn't look as Italian as my brother Tony and younger sisters, Joan and Ellen. I looked more like my mother's side, the Protestant, English side. I later validated this with my mother. She confirmed it was not just my imagination. She had the same perception and feelings.

Ave Maria

I know I sang Ave Maria,
In the garden early in the morning,
Tended olive trees
In pastel green fields,
Floated under the Blue Grotto.

I know I sang Ave Maria,
Lit candles
In a Catholic cathedral
At Nonno and Nonna's
Wedding and funerals.

I know I sang Ave Maria,
The beauty in the memory
Not the translation.

Moving to Maine

When I was eleven, my mother and father decided to build a house in Squantum, Massachusetts, where we had been renting a home. Papa did a lot of the construction himself. His cement mixer ran full tilt. I remember the beautiful stone wall he created. Although we lived in the house for two years before we moved to Maine, it was never completed.

Papa was always busy attending to his law practice and running for Selectman in Quincy. Mom spent her time with four children. She nearly went over the edge one Sunday when Papa was woodworking in the kitchen and three year old Steven picked up the power saw and almost severed his foot. Clara's husband Fred, a surgeon, worked on Steven's foot for six hours. He had to connect every tendon again. Steven was in the hospital for weeks and then in bed in a cast for a couple of months.

During this time Mom gave an ultimatum to Papa: "I'm moving to Maine with the children whether you come or not." Mom needed help taking care of us and my brother Steven. She was exhausted, mentally and physically. Nana Zottoli came to take care of us a couple of times.

In those days, the nineteen fifties, the husband usually was the one who earned the living and left the care of the house and children to the mother. Such was the case in our family. Mom needed help and her parents and Aunt Teddy, a nurse, who lived with my grandparents, filled that need.

So, we all moved to Brunswick, Maine, including Papa, and lived there for seven years in what we called, the "Big House." The Big House had been an inn many years before and my grandparents had made it into a working farm. My family moved in with them. There were six bedrooms and three bathrooms. It had a large barn and grazing fields. Seven of us, Mom, Papa, Tony, me, Joan, Steve and Ellen, who was born two years later, moved in and spread out in this large farmhouse. In the same year Ellen was born, 1953, my grandparents built a small home at the very end of Princes' Point. They had a view of the salt water, which went in and out with the tides over rocky shores and mudflats.

"The Big House" Farmhouse
Prince's Point Road, Brunswick, Maine, 1955
Papa's Buick and Grammy Macomber's Renault in the driveway.

Papa attempted to practice law in Brunswick, but did not do well, being an Italian in a French-Canadian town. He ended up returning to his practice in Quincy, working there during the week, and commuting home to Brunswick on the weekends. My father turned into a gentleman farmer when he was home on weekends and holidays, leaving Mom to see that the chores got done during the week.

My brothers and sisters and I helped Papa pitch hay, learned to drive on the tractor, and helped pull tree stumps in the sheep pasture. We rode in the hay wagon and slept in the hay loft. In the dark, imagining what was under the hay scared us, so we crept down into the house to sleep in our beds. Tony took care of the chickens and Steve tended the sheep. We had our blankets made from the wool. Joan cared for and rode a retired racehorse named Tallulah Bankhead.

Thanksgivings and Christmases with our grandparents in the Big House were wonderful. There were daiquiris, hors d' oeuvres, turkey, giblet gravy, pie, plum pudding (with flames) and games like Hide-the-Thimble, Up Jenkins and Charades. Grampa read selected portions of Dickens's *Christmas Carol*. As teens, we squirmed a bit, because we would rather have been with our friends.

In the winter, we skated on the pond. In the spring and fall, the woods rang with the sound of our voices as we played Robinson Crusoe, slide down the highest firs, or just rested on "moss hill." Grampa took us on nature walks and tried to teach us how to sail. In the summer, our cousins came from all over the country to visit. Together we swam from the boathouse and rowed and sailed in an inlet, we called "the reach." We played baseball in the field with our neighbors and did chores for our grandparents to earn money.

Mom and Papa inherited part of Grampa Macomber's property, Indian Point. Papa divided it and gave a building lot to each sister, and one to each of his five children. He always made sure his mother and sisters were taken care of financially and emotionally. His sisters, Clara and Kay, each built a summer cottage on their lots on the salt water. We did see them in summer, but had less contact with the Zottoli side the rest of the year.

My cousin, Mary Elaine, Clara's daughter, came to visit us one weekend. She brought a recording of Beethoven's *Fifth Symphony* with her. We had never been introduced to classical music. Mary put the record on and said, "We are all conductors," and proceeded to wave her arms to the music. We had such fun, our hands and feet going in all directions. Mom purchased a set of classical records at the grocery store the next week, and that began my love of Beethoven, Tchaikovsky and Mendelsohn.

When Papa came back to Maine on Friday nights, he often brought surprises. One time he brought a six month old Labrador retriever, Laddie, and one dozen chocolate éclairs, one for each of us and extras to be raffled. I felt left out when he brought home Mary Elaine's hand-me-downs. My Auntie Clara sent definite instructions that my sister Joan was to get the best ones. Because Joan was a tomboy, she dressed in my brother Tony's cast- offs. She still loves to get his older shamy shirts from L.L. Bean. Clara felt I was treated better, because I loved clothes and dressed better. She didn't realize it was because I earned and saved money just to get one article of nice clothing. The whole thing made me feel bad.

The Memory Ball

I am stuck in the memory ball
of the past. I sit on the deck
of my failing family cottage,
one of the last vestiges
of Grampa's compound.

I hear our voices
happy children
swimming and boating,
where we once ruled.
I walk by the barn
now in need of repair,
once vibrant with
chickens, sheep, steer,
the smell of new mown
hay wafting from the loft.

With memories' eyes
I see a grazing pasture, a haying field,
a picking place of blueberries
and wild strawberries,
now replaced by pines.

As I get older, I remember
the good memories.
They pass each other in the night.

Dear Papa

Before we moved to Maine, I didn't know my father very well. He was away from home most of the time, practicing law. I was shy in his presence and always tried to please him. In Maine, he was more relaxed, and the family had more quality time with him. We all farmed together on weekends and vacations. We loved his sense of humor and used to egg him on to tell fun incidents from the past.

Papa Robert Zottoli
At Grampa Macomber's house, Brunswick, ME, 1980s

Supper was a wonderful time at our house, full of laughter and conversation. We all had healthy appetites and took our share of food quickly or it would be gone. To avoid scuffles over who got what, Papa used the raffle method. For example: when there was an extra pork chop, piece of chicken, or an éclair, those wanting to be in the raffle picked a number from one to ten. The person choosing the number closest to the one Papa had in mind got the prize. Papa, the moderator, chuckled at the squeals of delight from the winner.

Salad was served at every supper. Papa poured the oil and vinegar from their bottles into the salad, which he then stirred in the same large aluminum pan. After years of use, the pan sprang a leak. Papa repaired the hole with a bolt and washer, and continued to use it. In my teen years when I had a friend for dinner, I asked beforehand if we could please use desert plates and a regular salad bowl that night.

Family Council Meeting was the time to make requests from the ridiculous to the sublime. "Will the meeting come to order," my father shouted. The excitement and laughter were stilled as the four children and two parents gleefully anticipated some fun. I laughed so hard I sometimes had to run to the bathroom. Joan read the secretary's report from the week before with a twinkle in her eyes. Requests such as putting a ban on the girls doing dishes and making beds and the boys not having to shovel manure were made only to be voted down. My mother refused to milk Katy, the cow, after the calf was born. Nobody else volunteered. This was very serious and resulted in the sale of dear Katrina. We all voted that Mom have another baby. The first motion by my brother Tony to close the meeting was denied, and so went joyful fun with Papa. My sister Ellen was born a year later.

Me and my brothers and sisters, 1955
Back row, Joan and Steve
Front row, Tony, Ellen, and Judith

Papa was a gentleman farmer. He loved working in the soil as did his father. In order to wean a calf from his mother and drink milk from a bucket, Papa attached a rubber hose to the bottom of the bucket. The calf sucked the hose and learned he was also drinking the milk. He patented the invention. Some years later, after the family had moved to Georgetown, Massachusetts, a suburban setting, Papa received a call from a farmer in Wisconsin. Two farmers in plaid shirts from cow country arrived in Georgetown wanting to buy the patent for five-hundred dollars. They were surprised to find a home with no barn, no farm, and no cows. Papa became known as "The Rubber Teat King."

In the same Georgetown house, Papa replaced the bathroom. My brother Steve worked with him on this long process. The glorious day arrived when the pipes were finally installed. Papa told Steve to shake the cold water pipe in the cellar so he would know where to hook up the hot and cold. We were at the supper table when Papa told Steve to go up and test the connections. All of a sudden Steve yelled, "There's steam coming out of the toilet."

A short time later, Papa installed sliding glass doors in the bathtub and shower. They were of the variety that you could see out from inside the shower, but no one could see you. Papa got ready to take the first shower, and shouted downstairs for us to come up and see this miraculous glass. As we entered the bathroom, we shrieked, "Papa, we can see you." He reversed the doors the next day.

Papa

Oh, the laughter,
the love and forgiving,
the sharing,
the giving,
nothing expected
in return.

Oh, the laughter
at the table,
the provider,
the counselor,
nothing expected
in return.

Oh, the laughter,
may it sound
in our minds
and hearts forever.
rest dear Papa,
your mission complete.

Robert Angelo Zottoli, 1938

My Dream of Italia

In 2005, my second husband Ed and I, whom I married in 1993, traveled to Italy to fulfill my dream of exploring where my family had come from. I wanted to find the town where Grampa Zottoli was born, to see where he walked the land and to absorb how he and his family lived and worked.

This constant yearning to capture my roots in no way diminishes the life experiences between our family's time in Maine and the fulfillment of my dream. During those forty or more years, I had two important careers, one as a wife, mother and grandmother, a second as a librarian. I'm blessed to have three beautiful children, Heidi, Kim and Mark and six wonderful grandchildren, William, Mary, Elizabeth, Daniel, Sascha and Joshua.

In 1982, my first husband, David, left me after nineteen years of marriage. I then had to support myself. Heidi and Kim were attending The Memorial University of Newfoundland. They had free tuition because David was a professor there. Mark lived with his father for two years while I went back to school. I had been going to night school during that first marriage and earned a B.A. in English and a B.Ed. in Education. After the divorce, I continued my education and attended Simmons College in Boston where I received my Masters in Library Science. I had a long and satisfying career as a librarian.

My children, Mark, Kim, and Heidi Watts, 1988

Judith and David Watt's grandchildren, 1999
Left to right, Joshua Hansen, Daniel Rasmussen, Elizabeth Goodwin,
Sascha Hansen, Mary Goodwin, William Goodwin

During these years my interest in my Italian heritage persisted. When I questioned some of my relatives, whether they had been to Sere where Grampa Zottoli was born, they answered, "No, it's probably a farm on a hill." These answers did not quell my desire to know more. I needed to belong to my Italian family. I continued to quiz the Zottolis and searched online for information and answers.

My great grandfather, Antonino Luciano Zottoli, was born in 1840 in the region of Campagnia, Italy. He married Carmella Dell' Aquila born in 1848 in Salerno. They prized education, were hard working and ambitious. They moved to Serre di Persano, Italy, a beautiful village in the mountains, where Grampa Zottoli was born. In Italy, when naming small villages, they put the larger municipality, where the town hall and officials reside, and then the village name. So Grampa Zottoli was born in Persano, about five kilometers west of Serre, or Serre di Persano.

At first Carmella was a teacher, but stayed at home when four sons came along. Because he felt his children would have more opportunities in America, Antonino emigrated from Italy to the North End in Boston, Massachusetts in 1882. He left Carmella and the four children in Serre until he could save enough money to bring them over too. Because he worked as a laborer his salary was not enough, so he learned how to use dynamite. He had to travel about to where they were blasting, but his new skill earned him an extra twenty-five cents an hour. Carmella and the four children sailed to Boston on the vessel *Italia* in 1884.

Antonino and Carmella Zottoli parented five more children in their new country, the United States.

Antonino's son, my grandfather, Anthony Michaelangelo Zottoli, became a sculptor and painter, working all over New England. He painted oil paintings of ships and flowers, studying art for seventeen years at night. He married Josephine Spera and they had four children. He had a studio in Scollay Square in Boston. Some of his brothers worked with him for a while as well as his children, Arthur, Robert and Clara. Although Anthony and Josephine placed importance on education for their children, Arthur, who died in his forties of tuberculosis, dropped out of high school and worked for his father. Clara became a librarian, Kay a librarian and my father Robert Angelo became a lawyer. In 1938 Robert married Jeanne Macomber who was a homemaker and an accomplished portrait painter.

On May 2, 2005, my long planned trip from the United States to Naples to Capri to Positano to Salerno and finally to Serre to find that "farm on the hill," where my grandfather Zottoli was born, became a reality.

The Dream

I long to know,
Italiano,
Campagnia,
Serre di Persano,
Mountains and fields,
Flowers and yields,
Blood of my birth,
Boots of my roots,
Passion of my soul,
Making me whole.

Blue Bus

"Mio nonno era nato een Serre, Mio Chiamo e Zottoli." "My grandfather was born in Serre, My name is Zottoli." I repeated the only Italian phrases I learned over and over again in Italy. The Italians knew why I was there.

On May 2, 2005, Ed and I flew from Portland, Maine to Boston, Massachusetts. After a long walk on tile and glass between Terminal A and E at Logan Airport, we boarded Alitalia at 4:40 P.M. My excitement ran high. Ed said my feet were three inches off the ground.

Alitalia was a great airline. The flight gave me a good feeling of what was to come in Italy. On board, we had a delicious meal, lively music and wine. There was a lot of turbulence and sleep did not come that night. The night disappeared with the clouds.

We arrived in Milan in the morning, our time, but afternoon theirs. Our next flight from Milan to Naples was delayed. After boarding the smaller plane we were asked to move to the back of the plane, as there was too much weight in the front to take off. It seemed suspicious as we were the only Americans and weighed much less than some others. The pilot walked on ahead of us sporting sneakers and an untucked shirt. As we walked across the tarmac to the plane, I saw him through the cockpit window with a large map spread out in front of him, my confidence waned.

After landing in Naples, we took a taxi from the airport to our hotel, San Francesco Al Monte. The taxi ride was unlike any I have ever had. Our cab joined the traffic of synchronous racecars going in the same direction and we were caught in the maze. We almost wiped out three people and two Vespas. The taxi driver said Naples was known for this.

The Hotel San Francesco Al Monte, formerly a convent, rose above Naples high on a hill. The rooms had high ceilings and nooks for statues. The rooftop was a beautiful garden with a waterfall, flowers, trees and shrubs surrounding it, all under the Mediterranean sun. Quite a contrast to the neighborhood below.

Napoli

I am here
Italia
Emotion
Overcomes.

The hills
Around Naples
Are misted
Not real.

Molto buono!
Mio nonno
Era nato
In Serre!

Bellissimo!

Naples, Italy, 2005

Judith and Ed Floyd in Naples, 2005

I couldn't wait to get out onto the streets of Naples. After checking into the hotel, we hurried outside to get a feel of the place. Just down the hill we found a restaurant serving pizza with buffalo cheese, delicious. Lunch over, we continued on the best we could. The streets were narrow, the Vespas fast and there were no sidewalks. The apartment buildings were at least three stories high with paint peeling and bright, white washing hanging on lines between buildings, a sharp contrast to the general dirty clutter below. I saw a well-dressed woman on her balcony, a red geranium at her feet, overlooking the scene.

Nonna

The old woman,
with white hair
in a bun,
stands on her balcony
in her finest indigo
dress, red geraniums
surrounding her.

The facade of her
apartment building:
peeling paint
on stucco.
She looks below
at life, a satisfied
expression
on her face.

The next day, May third, we got a taxi to the ferry landing to get a boat to the Isle of Capri. The driver almost wiped out a few more people. He said to leave the bags in the taxi, the meter still running, while I bought the tickets. There were two ferries waiting to make the trip. I bought the tickets and we went to board the remaining ferry. The captain said, "Your ticket is for the boat that just left." I had a minor breakdown, the Italian coming out. I cried, "*Mia nonno era nato een Serre*, I've been cheated, I've been cheated." The ferry captain saw my tears and without flicking an eyelash said, "You can ride on my ferry." I love Italy. Ed stood by saying to himself, "Who is this woman whose feet are ten inches off the ground?"

Isle of Capri, 2005

The ocean was calm, but for safety reasons we were ordered to stay inside the ferry. All of a sudden a huge rock, the size of a skyscraper, appeared not far from the boat. It was our destination, Capri. After landing, we took a taxi up the hill to where all the exclusive shops were. The only cars beyond this point were golf cart like vehicles which carry bus tour people, their luggage and supplies. We and our suitcases bumped over cobblestone streets for a mile to the Hotel Floridiana.

We were taken to our lovely hotel room with blue tile floors and a balcony overlooking the sea with terraced gardens and patios below filled with flowers. Yellow birds gathered in an apricot tree. Palm trees and pine trees lined the pathways where workers slowly climbed the hill beneath the mist covered high cliffs. We walked back to the area of shops to have lunch. Mealtimes are later in Italy, but worth the wait because the food is so delicious. Lunch is one-thirty to two-thirty and dinner around eight, which was an adjustment for us early risers. We ate lots of pizza, pasta, fish, salad, gelato, and drank strong coffee and wine.

The next day we went to Positano by boat. The ferry left at three in the afternoon and we had to be out of the hotel by twelve, so we pulled our luggage up a cobbled incline to an outdoor café, where we had lunch. We then took the cable car down the hill and sat on cement steps, people watching, boatload after boatload of tourists arriving.

We landed on the beach at Positano. A platform, ten or twelve feet long, was lowered from the ferry to the beach. We were met on the beach by a rough looking group of workmen who spoke to us in Italian. Not knowing what to say I tried "*Quanto costa.*" He answered ten to which I told him O.K. We looked up at the most beautiful sight, a town built into a hill.

We ended up sitting in the back of a pick-up truck belonging to the workman who quoted the price. The way up the mountain was a service road with water running down it under us. Ed sat on the side of the truck, his back pack scraping the rocks on the side of a tunnel. Finally, we reached the top and our hotel. The Positea, a Best Western, was very nice with a balcony overlooking the Mediterranean and the town of Positano. The houses appeared to be glued to the mountain.

On the warm, sunny, fifth day of our trip, we were still in Positano. As John Steinbeck said of this Italian village on a hill, "Positano bites deep. It is a dream place that isn't quite real when you are there and becomes beckoningly real after you have gone." Life there is vertical. We walked down hundreds of cement steps from the hotel to the bottom. Along the way we passed cats, kittens, people going to work and lovely doorways built into the hill and adorned with flowers.

Positano

I sit on my balcony
looking down at
layer upon layer
of freshly painted
stucco hotels, next
to peeling ,dirty
homes, hanging
from the rock
above the sea.
People walk
the narrow road
below, the well
dressed tourist,
next to the drab
workman with paint
on his trousers.

Positano, Italy, 2005

When we reached the bottom, I got my feet wet in the cold Mediterranean Sea. The beach glass in shades of blue and green was just as enticing as at home. We went shopping along the boardwalk, where I tried bartering for a skirt and blouse. The shop owner looked amused when I told her I was expected to try negotiating. She smiled and came down ten euros. The weather was cool for May so we stopped at a café that had windows open to the sea, but a heater at our feet. We had the best lemon cake ever made from local lemons. That night we hired Flavio Gioia to drive us along the Amalfi Coast to Salerno in his Mercedes Benz taxi.

May seventh, the next morning, we left Positano and had a delightful ride on narrow winding roads with breathtaking views of the azure sea from the top of rocky cliffs. In the distance we saw Sorento, Mount Versuvius and Pompei. Flavio, I love to say his name, drove us to the Jolly Hotel in Salerno. We walked around town and stopped in a market and bought cheese, salami and bread for our lunch.

Promenade in Salerno, 2005

Salerno is at the base of mountains and is very flat. It has a stone promenade along a pebble beach lined with palm trees. Feeling safer here than Naples, we walked the promenade and through the park amongst lovers, venders and families. We passed gathering spots where young and old friends met, and loved ones enjoyed the sunny day. Older men gathered around cement tables to play cards. That evening we had a glass of wine and the most delicious green olives, direct from the trees. For dinner, I had *Antipasto Mare* (squid) and Ed had *Crostini Salmone* with a good wine and bread. After dinner we sat on a bench on the promenade and people watched; my favorite pastime.

The next day, Sunday, was the day I dreamed about, to find Serre. Because of the language barrier, I could find no one who knew which bus went to Serre. We had just about given up when we asked a driver waiting with his bus. He said, "You take that blue bus behind me." We were on our way.

Serre

The hills beyond
Like patchwork quilts
Uniform rows
Olives, lemons.

The wedding parade
Winds through streets
Honking horns
Cellphones to ears.

My family gone
From red roof home;
Spirits persist
For many years.

I carry the love,
Laughter and tears
In heart and soul
Through life everlasting,

Generation to generation…

Countryside of Serre, Italy, 2005

The countryside was beautiful going up into the hills, full of olive and lemon trees neatly in rows of lush green. A company that made red tiles, another that made cement statues and the one that ran the blue buses were along the way. The town was spotless; the old part with its cobble streets and old stone buildings being restored. In the center was the original church, tall and inspiring. Men gathered in the square to talk and play cards while the women went to church and prepared dinner. Most of the shops were closed, but one was open, and the owner spoke English. I repeated to anyone who would listen, *"Mio chiamo e Zottoli, mio nonno era nato een Serre."* Nobody knew the name Zottoli.

As we were sitting in the square, we saw a mother and three small children run to greet a nun who gathered them in her arms. The church, both old and new, is a strong fabric of Serre. Because it was Sunday we could not look at the records for the Zottoli family. The newer part of Serre had modern homes and in the distance there was an apartment complex run by wind power.

As we waited on a bench for the blue bus to take us back to Salerno, I watched a *Nonna*, stoic, loving, wise, the person I would like to be. A wedding procession of cars passed twice with horns beeping and people waving, circling through the town. At a table outside a restaurant nearby was a group of elderly men. I went over and said "*Mio chiamo e Zottoli.*" One man said there are no Zottolis left.

I looked out the window of the blue bus as we drove away from Serre and the elderly man waved to me. I waved back with tears in my eyes. I knew why the Zottolis left and yet I didn't. My ancestors were part of the town over one hundred years ago. My footprints remain.

The next day, we took the train back to Naples. We took a taxi to the Archeological Museum only to find it was closed on Mondays. We had to cross a major street with double two-way traffic, no traffic lights or cross walks and stood there in bafflement. A third *Nonna* took us each by the elbow and walked us across the traffic which stopped inches from us. The drivers gave us thumbs up. We all hugged. A *Nonna* is to me, what I had hoped and believed Nana to be: wise, merry and loving.

We flew home to Boston the next day. I love you Italia. You are part of me. I belong with you.

Old church in Serre, 2005

Street scene in old Serre, Italy, 2005

Italia

I claim you *Italia*
my ancestors before.
You give me a passion
that excites and restores.

I search for a mountain
where *Nonno* once plowed
grateful and thankful
my being's allowed.

I live in *Italia*
my spirits from past.
I am emotion
accepted at last.

I sing in my garden
barefoot on earth
mother of three
celebrated since birth.

Notes

Made in the USA
Charleston, SC
02 December 2012